The Haters

The
Haters

AARON SIMMONS JR

PALMETTO

P U B L I S H I N G

Charleston, SC

www.PalmettoPublishing.com

Hardcover ISBN: 9798822956636

Paperback ISBN: 9798822956643

eBook ISBN: 9798822956650

The
Haters

AARON SIMMONS JR

PALMETTO

PUBLISHING

Charleston, SC

www.PalmettoPublishing.com

Hardcover ISBN: 9798822956636

Paperback ISBN: 9798822956643

eBook ISBN: 9798822956650

Summary

We who are descendants of slaves, labor to not stoop to the level of cruelty that we endure and do so for the promise of a better life after our death. There is a sense of urgency and desperation in the people of America because the idea of an authoritarian regime is being entertained by popular would-be presidents who aspire to moonlight as dictators.

Introduction

It happened so often that it seemed to be a sport. The lynchings recorded in the United States between the Reconstruction era and the present-day number over four thousand. The unfathomable atrocities that were perpetrated upon innocent people can't be justified—not that anyone has tried. Politicians are proclaiming a platform of law and order in the year 2022. This is after there is nothing left to steal and plunder from the indigenous people who have suffered gross indignities: thousands of their ancestors' graves have been desecrated, and their bodies are now showcased in museums. Is one of them not like the others—or not human? My answer is atrociously no! It was not enough to greedily consume the food; the plunderers decided to lick the pot by stealing the bodies of the victims and their artifacts!

The same plunderers that are responsible for the downfall of the indigenous people of America also enslaved African Americans in this land of the free. We who are descendants of slaves, labor to not stoop to the level of cruelty that we endure and do so for the promise of a better life <u>after</u> death. This promise was born out of the hopelessness of an oppressed people. The former slaves who worked under the cruel treatment of the slave master are mercifully gone from this earth—but their children still labor for every ounce of freedom and dignity. Now with the new pillars of power in place within the super-majority-laden Supreme Court, and the promise to form a raw and cruel leadership if the far-right-wing politicians can win control of Congress, sons and daughters of former slaves will be facing a new threat to their quest for equality.

The 2022 midterm election is at hand, and the future of democracy is uncertain. There is a sense of urgency and desperation in the people of America because the idea of an authoritarian regime is being entertained by popular would-be presidents who aspire to moonlight as dictators. There are many supporters of this movement. It is also sanctioned by some Christian denominations—promoting the cause of Christian White nationalism. Inevitably, the decline of human rights and dignity will follow if we are left to the ideology of the descendants of slave owners, themselves responsible for the first wave of tyranny upon people of color during and after slavery.

Not long ago, lynchings were commonplace in America. That wound has not healed...

Book One

Chapter One:
Willie Lynch

He has been attributed a sordid history. His legacy should be written in blood, if it can be authenticated. "The infamous letter of Willie Lynch" has been debated, and its authenticity has been disputed for centuries. I will attempt to show the juxtaposition of its incidental relevance to the suffering souls who were recipients of the hell that it was said to have promised and the evidence presented by critics for the timing of incidents written about in the letter not to be possible within the time in history that it was written. I will start with the strategies that Willie Lynch supposedly outlined to the slave owners as a method to control their slaves.

In strategy one, attributed to the infamous speech before the American slave owners, Willie Lynch extolls the art of breeding the Black slave women with the slave owners to obtain a desirable skin color. This process would alienate the true thoroughbred lineage of the Africans. The multiple crossbreedings could produce a multiplicity of colors. Although we are of many shades of color today, dear reader, we all identify as "Black" because we understand the past process of crossbreeding our people. What seems to be a paradox of sorts is that these descendants of slave owners would be brothers and sisters to each other. Furthermore, the unspeakable is that they would be the slave owners' own children.

The futility of the effort to steer clear of miscegenation and maintain a lily-white race is laughable under such a ridiculous scenario. The unlaughable part is that we were subjected to a loss of our identity through such incidental crossbreeding. Did the resulting genetic makeup also become a collage of brotherhood within the newfound kinship? Did they produce a person who was at conception already confused and worthy of psychological evaluation with the conflicting ideology of "I came, I saw, I conquered," as stated by the European Eric the Red, as opposed to "We shall overcome someday"? The genetic makeup of a mixed-race individual had little to do with the rigors of the life of an enslaved person, beyond the <u>misinformation</u> that was used by the slave owner to exploit the pigmentation of the skin to his advantage. Thus, "White is all right, Brown stick around, Black stay back." This assertion does seem to support the claim by Willie Lynch that there <u>are</u> many shades of Black and White people. It does <u>not</u> authenticate the so-called contribution by Willie Lynch of an orchestrated crossbreeding of slaves. It could have been a simple act of unmitigated rape by the slave owners.

Strategy two of Willie Lynch's alleged slave controlling plan involves denying the slaves access to the understanding of the English language. This process would guarantee that the slave would forever be a fool in a foreign land. Thus it was a crime for a slave to read and write the English language.

Strategy three: instilling the concept of differences in the makeup of the slaves through misinformed suggestions fed to them. These differences included skin color, denoting inferior or superior status. Age was used, as well as factors that denoted appearance, such as coarse hair and size, to promote envy and confusion among the slaves.

I have seen this practice in the twentieth century. The legacy of Willie Lynch's so-called lessons to the slave owners smacks of a reality that has been alive and well throughout the history of the African American experience in the United States. The whip and the chains were only part of the breaking of the slave. The control of a person's destiny through ignorance by denial of education meant almost total control of a person's existence. Without referencing further examples of "the infamous Willie Lynch letter," it is possible to glean from the above methods of slave control that we have been handled with a concerted effort toward dehumanization of our people. In no other culture in this land of the free has a people been so cruelly treated. The beat goes on, for we are still the recipients of the most hate crimes in America.

Now the question becomes, did Willie Lynch create all this hell single-handedly? Did he create any of it? I must agree with the critics who doubt the authenticity of a so-called letter by Willie Lynch, but I will authenticate the methods of slave control, because remnants of the slave treatment remain until this day. The lynchings of Black Americans—the term itself his namesake—is another story. Why is the practice called "lynching," after him, when his so-called speech was against the practice of lynching? It is his alleged speech to the slave owners, rather than a mystical letter, that gives lie to the authenticity of the story. The elephant in the room is the poor Black people who suffered under the hatred of the cruel oppressors. The haters didn't need instructions from

anyone to carry out some of the most heinous crimes involving the lynchings of our people.

The following truth is an account by an NAACP investigator named Walter White who investigated forty-one lynchings between 1918 and 1927. Note the NAACP describes a lynching thus: "a public execution of an individual who has not received any due process."

The Lynching of Mary Turner
May 19, 1918, Georgia

Abusive plantation owner Hampton Smith was shot and killed. A week-long manhunt resulted in the killing of Mary Turner's husband, Hayes Turner. Mary denied that her husband had been involved in Smith's killing, publicly opposed her husband's murder, and threatened to have members of the mob arrested. On May 19, 1918, a mob of several hundred brought her to Folsom Bridge, tied Mary's ankles, hung her upside down from a tree, doused her in gasoline and motor oil and set her on fire. She was still alive when a member of the mob split her abdomen open with a knife. Her unborn child fell to the ground, stomped and crushed. Mary's body was riddled with hundreds of bullets.

Such were the unbridled lynchings of African Americans throughout our odyssey in this land of the free.

The alleged presentation of Willie Lynch to the plantation owners pales by comparison. The juxtaposition is clear. The theft of a person's mind and humanity is egregious beyond repair, but the monstrous deeds committed on Black people by lynching them were too inhumane for understanding. The hatred is demonic at best. Not since hell was created in American folklore has anything real been identified that came close to comparing. This land of the free has come a long way from those days of mass lynchings, but the struggle is not over.

Chapter Two:
Woke

The dictionary defines "woke" as "alert to injustice in society—especially to racism." Someone is trying to pass laws against <u>wokeness</u>. As a dam is a stalwart barrier against too much water, these policies are designed to make the victim <u>dumb—back</u> to the era of Jim Crow—still asleep to the extremist ideology that is seeking absolute power. "Absolute" in this context means authoritarianism.

A fascist is someone who supports or promotes fascism, a system of government led by a dictator who typically rules forcefully and violently, suppressing opposition and criticism, controlling all industry and commerce, and promoting nationalism and racism. The similarities to the antiwoke policies are striking.

There is an evil force that has a grip on the American dream, as African Americans struggle to survive. It seems to have a stranglehold on our advances. I deem this evil force to be hate.

Hate is like a filthy rag that's used to clean the kennels of a thousand hounds of hell. A filthy rag then brought into the house as a trophy—not unlike the head of a hapless moose that might adorn the wall of a proud hunter. There it might rest as a memorial, to a dank, cruel captain of a four-hundred-year-old slave ship that still sails on an imaginary Atlantic Ocean, with its pitiful cargo of souls, who are predestined for centuries of antiwoke laws and merciless torture by merciless slave owners and antiwoke lawmakers.

The antiwoke law is steeped and sautéed in a wicked, witchlike craft that was handed down from the period of Reconstruction as a potion against the struggle that the freedmen are forever mounting.

This craft was the mother of Jim Crow and was called the "black codes." They were designed to rob Black people of their freedom by using antiwoke law, which denied quality education and voting rights to the newly freed freedmen, as they were called by the Union. Now these black codes are being used as a wolfsbane kind of guard against wokeness or maybe a reinforced padlock that can prevent the opening of a Pandora's box of sorts, filled with a historic trove of precious atrocities. Desperate measures are being taken by the haters to prevent exposure of these hidden artifacts, lest young eyes behold them and are awakened from their slumber.

The antiwoke hater is using millions of taxpayer dollars to attack minority groups with a vindictive and vengeful aggression. We are also faced with law enforcement haters. These haters stalk their victims—which is to say, these racist policemen murder black people—and apologize with millions of dollars, while the antiwoke movement stealthily uses Jim Crow lies as a blindfold against the sordid revelations of a shameful past.

These lies paint a portrait of hypocrisy that places the victim of the lies in a reverse role, thereby depicting him as the evil perpetrator. So skillful are the liars who tell these lies that if they were oil-on-canvas paintings, they would be worthy of comparison to Picasso.

These racist lies that frame our quest for equality as a political ideology were born from the putrid carcass of a selfish ideology known as nationalism and were just one pup from a litter that also birthed the business of people for profit, as in chattel slavery. They are the children of hate.

Exactly one hundred years ago, on January 1, 1923, an angry <u>mob</u> of White citizens destroyed Rosewood, a Black community in Florida, and killed some of its inhabitants. Now in the year 2023, on the anniversary of this hideous act, no mention is made by the state of Florida, which instead wages war on the so-called <u>woke</u> <u>mob</u> if they dare to talk about such history. Someone in a powerful position is painting the portrait that was mentioned earlier, for gullible eyes to behold and to be fearful of.

The craft called "antiwoke," borrowed from old Jim Crow, is rife with deceit. Lawsuits have been filed by more than one group challenging the onslaught against First Amendment rights under the United States Con-stitution, which promises free speech. Corporate Amer-ica is also under attack from political populists because of the woke agenda, which they are indoctrinating into their training.

The noose of authoritarianism is subtly tightening around democratic America in opposition to minority rights. The entire ideology of <u>equality and freedom from systemic injustice</u>, aka <u>racism</u>, is under attack. The state of Florida is leading the charge, and with a newly elect-ed GOP majority in the US House of Representatives, accompanied by a super majority of conservatives on the SCOTUS, a hot bed of challenges awaits our weary children of former slaves in the year 2023.

There is also a newly prominent right-wing populist that must be mentioned in this thrust toward woke-busting. We would like to introduce an authoritarian president from across the sea: Victor Orbán was the keynote speaker at the Conservative Political Action Conference on August 4, 2022. He is the president of Hungary, and his policies have been closely and conspicuously mirrored by the state of Florida on matters such as LGBTQ rights and critical race theory. Punishment for Disney reflects Orbán's style of authoritarian government by using powers invested by the people to further a far-right agenda—and enacting laws that enforce this agenda. Any objections to these policies are punished. This agenda is ruthless in its effort to declare war on minority advances. These advances are pronounced discriminatory in simple, benevolent projects such as the aim of the NHL to recruit black hockey players.

Gerrymandering during Florida's midterm elections was another weapon that reflected Orbán's style. Districts were reformed in such a way as to completely eradicate the strength of minority voting blocks, thereby effecting an outcome that was favorable for the right-wing conservative group.

The platform is also dangerous in that it follows a pattern that Adolf Hitler used to kill six million Jews. The banning of books is very <u>dictator-like</u> in nature. It assures that a person is asleep to the ugly actions of dictators. The state of Florida is banning books that expose systemic racism in our educational foundation.

Chapter Three:
Deception

If antiwoke is a product of hate, then deceit is fruit from the same family tree. Some of our foremost dedicated freedom-seekers—W. E. B. Dubois, Booker T. Washington, and Monroe Trotter—were deceived by the promises of then US president Woodrow Wilson (*Berkeley Haas News*, "How Woodrow Wilson's Racist Policies Eroded the Black Civil Service"). Excerpts from the above article evince the misinformation that can deceive the savviest of us with the cunning guile of a deceptive mind. Woodrow Wilson's promise to champion civil service advances for minorities in government jobs was a ploy to pull black votes away from the Republican party. He then launched an all-out racist campaign against minorities by first filling his cabinet with Southern Democrats who would enforce racist policies, such as firings and demotions of Blacks in civil service jobs.

Woodrow Wilson's segregation policies were a master deception. Their effects are still being felt in the twenty-first century. Not only did Black Americans get the worst setback in employment in civil service jobs since Reconstruction, but there were also more lynchings of African Americans during his terms in the White House than at any other period after Reconstruction (NAACP). This was because he was indifferent to the treatment that Black people were receiving from racist Whites during this onslaught of terrorism.

It was during Woodrow Wilson's tenure that W. E. B. Dubois, who was editor of *The Crisis*, published a photo essay called "The Waco Horror" that showed the horrible image of a seventeen-year-old Black teenager named Jesse Washington being lynched in Waco, Texas. Mr. W. E. B. Dubois was truly a courageous champion of freedom during this period, while Mr. Woodrow Wilson was certainly a master deceiver. The image of Jesse Washington displayed in the NAACP chronicles brought about the memory of an incident in my childhood that will forever be a wake-up call.

He (I) was rudely awakened in the year 1957. That year he was twelve years old. He had harbored a false sense of security until he was jolted by reality while strolling down US Highway 90. The heavy vehicle that was approaching him may have been an Oldsmobile or a Pontiac, but what he remembered most was the loud and raucous voices that shouted racial epithets from the car. "Get that little nigger!"

He remembered the car swinging around into a U-turn as he started to swiftly run to safety. He scampered behind the warehouses, where his father had fired the big boilers, which supplied steam to radiators for rich white folks who lived in the downtown area. He could hear the drunken shouting of the men in the heavy car as they looked for him along the dusk-dark street.

He didn't know that Emmett Till had been lynched two years earlier or that there were people who would do something so evil to a child—nor why they would. He had never heard grown men express such animosity toward a child before then.

He picked his way through the warehouses—being ever careful not to expose himself to the hostility that was now associated with Highway 90 in his twelve-year-old mind. He made his way through thick underbrush to a familiar neighborhood where he knew that his older sister was visiting with friends. He had survived.

This is a true incident from my childhood, but now, as I write about it, the incident weighs more horribly than in 1957 because at this time, my seventy-seven-year-old legs would not have allowed me to escape. Jesse Washington of Waco Texas did not. NAACP files chronicle the lynching of Jesse Washington in the year of our Lord 1916, and it happened during the deceitful tenure of the Honorable Woodrow Wilson. Washington was a seventeen-year-old Black teen lynched in Waco, Texas, by a white mob that accused him of killing Lucy Fryer, a white woman.

During our infinite struggle for the right to merely survive in America, a great deal of our people have been killed because of instances that involve the age-old false premise of "a monster of a Black man dared to desire a White woman!" She recognizes the power of life and death that she holds due to the utterly despicable cruelty perpetrated on innocent Black citizens, and in more recent years she has been inclined to call the police on innocent people such as when Amy Cooper reported false charges against Christian Cooper, a Black man in Central Park. Although she was arrested, charges were later dropped against her. She stated that she was going to call the police and tell them that an African American had threatened her life. The video in which she was seen speaking the false threats may have saved Christian

Cooper's life. America has set a dangerous precedent of unmitigated genocide upon Black men for White women to exploit.

I look at this situation as something that I call "carefree racism," deceitful in its appearance because it sometimes comes disguised behind a mask worn by people who aren't trustworthy. A White congresswoman is called upon to honor copyright law. She then berates the owner of the copyrighted materials, who is Black, with stereotypical accusations, such as unproven drug use and thug-labeling false innuendoes. These acts of hate describe a person that is carefree in their racist world, knowing that the world in which she lives will protect the status quo of hundreds of hate-filled years for people of color. She is saying, "I can break the law—if I'm breaking it against a Black person." This apology is unacceptable! The antiwoke campaign is also unacceptable! It is a preparation for a larger campaign of larceny of our civil rights. It does not come in the form of a masked burglar in the still of the night but in the form of an indignant victim of an imaginary crime that was committed by people of color who only wanted to "let freedom reign"!

In the year 2023, some of the elected officials of government were expressing the ideology of the haters in American society. While they spout freedom from deceptive lips, their quest for freedom is a red herring, offered as an <u>alternative fact</u> to the true provisions of the US Constitution, which is in direct opposition to the antiwoke charade. As this antiwoke case goes before the US Supreme Court, we will get the opportunity to witness the court's intent as to whether it will remain steadfast in its theme of <u>textualism</u>. If this happens, then the court will uphold the promise of life, liberty, and the pursuit of happiness, which has nothing to do with "I want you to be devoid of the truth in America."

Populism is a fearful trend in American politics when a populist tends to appease his political base without rational consideration for the consequences of his actions. The quest for the right to freedom is being extinguished by the power of the elite, overriding the will of the common citizen by buying up politicians who are willing to step on the laws that protect our democratic values, such as the onslaught against the First Amendment.

I am reminded of a time when I was a local union president. There were negotiations of contracts and grievance procedures to deal with in the process of running a union. It was a survival-of-the-fittest kind of skirmish for the rank and file. The company doesn't want to be challenged on anything. Statements such as "I am doing this hardship to you, but what are you going to do about it?" were common in our talks with them. The state of Florida, with its <u>reverse racism</u> approach to anything that might advance the progress of African Americans, has declared our advances to be racist. Openly and blatantly, they are arbitrarily singling out minority programs to make racist laws against, while ignoring European programs to enforce the slogan "White is all right, Black stay back," and this time, "Brown go down." This is the same as "I am making laws to hurt you, but what are you going to do about it?" If it seems to be too extreme, it's because it is designed to satisfy extremists. It is amazing how popular these neo–Jim Crow laws are with White America. We are neither mute nor amazed, for the outcry against this stomping and tromping upon our First Amendment rights is being heard from coast to coast in the United States.

I have acquaintances, from across the track, who have tried to convince me that Florida's bogus policies will only be against Hispanic people and that, therefore, I should vote for this would-be dictator who is building a platform for the office of POTUS by making state laws that will eradicate our rights as citizens. It is tantamount to telling us that we cannot learn. This is not the first time in modern times that laws have been made in a bold and aggressive affront to our rights. Every one of us needs to take a stand verbally against this intent to rewrite Black history—to whitewash the truth about our burden in America. This is not the time to bury our heads in the sands of sorriness but to stand tall and earn the admiration that we deserve, in honor of those who have given their lives so that we can enjoy the fruits of liberty promised in the creed of the United States Constitution.

The intended incarceration of our rights is pressing against the very liberty and well-being of Black children who are not yet born, to the extent that the black codes adopted in the era of Reconstruction could easily become the misinformation that our future children would be exposed to. This would be possible under the act proposed by the state of Florida to ban any book that gives a true account of our history. There is not a great deal of deception here. This is a concerted effort to resurrect another wave of oppression on our people. It should convince someone to go to the polls and vote. Remember this: deception is a wrecking ball used by Old Jim Crow to tear your house of freedom down.

There are wrecking balls enough to tear down our sanctuaries of liberty, but we do not expect that someone who looks like us can be blind to the reality of what's happening—unless they aren't blind at all. They may be master deceivers.

There is a former secretary of state who is on the soapbox preaching against critical race theory. She has said that her parents taught her racism was not her problem. She has also said that White people should not be made to feel guilty about past deeds perpetrated upon Black people. Ms. Rice, we commend you for your success as a political icon, but I must condemn your chosen position against the struggle of Black people through centuries of police brutality; inferior learning institutions; unequal pay for equal production; "last hired, first fired" practices in the workplace; lynchings of Black people (which are still going on today); Jim Crow voter restrictions against Black citizens that are growing more prevalent in today's climate and reached great heights during your term as Secretary of State.

I am asking you to please give us some history of your doing anything to correct any of the above infractions against our people. Your bread is out of the oven and has been buttered quite nicely. You could have chosen to remain silent as you always have when these injustices were in front of you, but you have mounted a rebuttal against the struggle. The point of making White people feel guilty about their dastardly deeds is miniscule in comparison to the deeds that they are still committing against us. The "stop woke act" isn't some imaginary law but a real thrust toward rewriting the history of our struggle in America. You should have remembered your parents' teachings that "Racism isn't your problem"!

An aspiring White nationalist would naturally try to kill any study that would expose the vulnerable underbelly of racism. The very act of designing laws to outlaw the inquisition of the truth about institutional racism supports the need for Jim Crow to disavow critical race theory. Again, we are neither mute—nor amazed. The greatest lie that is being told is that our quest for equality, and the desire to be treated in a humane fashion, is just a political ideology. We will not be sidetracked by political jargon that is a carefully designed, racist, and mean-spirited vehicle to reach a plateau of authoritarian autocracy.

Chapter Four:
The Super Bigots

———————◆———————

The dictionary defines *bigot* as "a person who is obstinately or <u>unreasonably</u> attached to a belief, opinion, or faction, especially one who is prejudiced against or <u>antagonistic toward a person or people</u> on the basis of their membership of a particular group" (emphasis added). One such example of bigotry is the practice of <u>redlining</u>.

Redlining can be defined as a discriminatory practice that consists of the systematic denial of services such as mortgages, insurance loans, and other financial services to residents of certain areas based on their race or ethnicity. This practice is the work of super bigots, so called because <u>their</u> bigotry has the power to create conditions of hardship for innocent citizens. Some popular and familiar entities were exposed by the Justice Department as they went about the business of trampling on our quest for a level playing field in the fair housing arena, as well as our ability to obtain loans from banks, comparable insurance rates, and other commodities that we need as compensation for our loyalties to this country. There are also super bigoted state governments enacting super bigoted state laws against our progress, such as banning books that tell the truth about redlining, and other bigoted infractions against us, but we are grateful that there is a higher law that rests in the US Constitution—and is being exercised to uncover these super bigoted redliners. I do not believe that this struggle will end soon. The Civil War was unsuccessful in ending the hatred. It is as American as baseball, hot dogs, apple pie, and Chevrolet.

This is the America that we all pledge allegiance to, as do "useful idiots" posing as patriots while striving for power to further enact White supremacist ideologies. Useful idiot in this context is not meaning naïve or subject to manipulation by foreign dictators, as the term was used by the Soviet dictator Lenin in 1864, but more of an opportunist that can cleverly pose as a useful idiot while drinking from a bitter cup of autocracy and from a sweet cup of democracy simultaneously.

The confusion is savored by some white-collar businesses in America—themselves traditional redliners—in keeping with the crafts of the <u>black codes</u> from the Reconstruction era, while throwing riches at this neo–Jim Crow who promises to continue the destruction of our freedom in exchange for overflowing coffers. The businesses may perceive this new Jim Crow as their useful idiot who can provide new opportunities for redlining. The poor people pray for salvation, while the wolf is preying on the poor people's situation with <u>misinformation</u> and <u>disinformation</u>.

Redlining isn't the only tool used by bigots to hate and oppress minorities, however. Gentrification is a big weapon against acquisition or ownership of property by minorities. The mother of all gentrifications on American soil happened when the west was so-called won. Isn't that what Vladimir is doing in Ukraine? The killing went on until the reservations were filled with Native Americans. The plundering of artifacts and theft of bodies is a sore topic today. "Alternative truths" about this travesty are being told—that <u>repatriations</u> are forthcoming; but can repatriations repair the bogus gentrification upon a people and their nations? Again, there is nothing left to steal. Americans proudly honor this conquest of innocent people and even praise the ones who resisted (Geronimo). Many suffered in horrible fashion.

One ordeal was deemed the Trail of Tears and was endured by Indians and African Americans alike. The minister of this pain is on the front of the twenty-dollar bill, with our greatest Black female warrior <u>cast</u> upon the back as a symbol of a subordinate to a great torturer. The recognition and attempt to mitigate the effects of the Trail of Tears horror by removing remnants of slavery have created a backlash that has led at least one state of Florida lawmaker to introduce legislation that, if passed, would eliminate the entire Democratic party. The noose of bigotry would tighten not-so-subtly with such a bold thrust toward a neo–Jim Crow government. These hideous attempts at legislation are passed off by some as a political stunt to garner votes, but there is a welcoming host of bigots interested in this ideological context. The platform is pure bigotry.

Gentrification is as or even more prevalent today. It is possible through the government's right to eminent domain (the Fifth Amendment). There may be complicity, by the state of Florida, in one such case involving a century-old Black community. The recipients who will benefit are White business owners seeking to get an interstate highway built through a Black community. This would destroy the history and any property value of the community. It would be a clear case of gentrification being used in a bigoted fashion.

There should be no doubt about the intentions and the efforts to short-circuit the advancements of African Americans in this land of opportunity. History is testament to the many ways of discrimination, which include concerted bigoted programs such as disinformation by the elected officials in the realm of educating our children; redlining of citizens from minority groups to curtail the acquiring of a quality livelihood; as well as gentrification. Redlining can be said to extend into the medical arena, where it is telling that Black women and their babies die at a much greater rate than their counterparts due to denial of quality prenatal care. If that is not enough bigotry—the prison system is stocked with African Americans who are more likely to be given harsher sentences for the same crimes as are committed by their White counterparts.

No one is denying these truths, while many are doubling down on the infractions. The idea is to issue disinformation about the purpose of our desire to expose the true history of our quest for freedom and equality, as well as the inhumane treatment along the way. The disinformation paints a picture of White people being mistreated through falsehoods that are <u>said</u> to reflect America's history. Again, we are neither mute nor amazed.

I would like to present a group of warriors who need no introduction. Their work speaks for itself, and it is now the bane of right-wing conservatives. They gave us critical race theory.

***

Critical race theory is the super bigot's nemesis!

A culmination of inquisitions would naturally lead to the conclusions from the brilliant minds of Kimberle Crenshaw, Derrick Bell, Alan Freeman, Richard Delgado, Cheryl Harris, Charles R. Lawrence III, and Patricia J. Williams that our own legal system could be complicit in the unequal treatment of minorities through a <u>convenient</u> entanglement of policies that gives priority to certain laws over our civil rights.

We celebrate and welcome the work that you have prepared for us, for it is a brilliant guideline to shed light upon the unbalanced playing field that we must negotiate while we journey to a kinder, gentler existence in this potentially greater nation. Your work leaves no reason to be critiqued because the response to your opinion is as telling as the cliché "the cat is out of the bag." This is evidenced by the banning of books in our public schools and the attempt to shortstop your efforts to enlighten us in the ways that Jim Crow is being used to hurt us. I am convinced that this silver bullet will pierce the armor of so-called originalism and textualism that coconspirators in neo–Jim Crow are hiding behind.

Ms. Kimberle Crenshaw asked a very important question as we citizens of the state of Florida witnessed the attack upon our schools and universities. "Are schools on the side of the neo-segregationist faction? Or are they going to stick with the commitments that we've all celebrated for the last fifty, sixty years?" The answer, in my opinion, is somewhere in the halls of the SCOTUS.

Mr. Derrick Bell, who pioneered critical race theory, is a true warrior who possesses an appetite for social justice. Along with the valiant crew that was named earlier, I salute these present-day activists for justice and equality.

Before I introduce another freedom fighter, there is an observation that I would like to share with you. From the moment African Americans set foot in these United States, they were slaves, mistreated and made to be commodities for the growth of America—they were chattel slaves. It is super gross to think that the father of America would pluck a black man's teeth out and put them in his own mouth and eat with them. A black chattel slave would be helpless to stop him! Historical records show that on May 8, 1784, he paid six pounds, two shillings to "negroes for 9 teeth on account of the French Dentist Doctor Lemay." History has more accounts of his wooden teeth than the teeth of slaves, but a preponderance of the evidence is cloudy after 239 years have passed. Would a slave owner buy commodities from a slave that he owned? Such treatment is a reason to have school children hate their foreparents.

At this time, I would like to honor Ms. Nicole Hannah-Jones, who is the author of the 1619 Project. The power of her work has caused the forty-fifth president to issue an executive order. The Advisory 1776 Commission is supposed to be a response to the 1619 Project. A real response should be an apology and, if sincere, reparations. Instead, we got threats to cut funding from schools that had lessons about the 1619 Project. From this threat came the Advisory 1776 Commission. Its real mission, in my opinion, is to substitute "alternative facts" for the true history of slavery and other wrongs that were committed against African Americans from the year 1619 until the present day.

The banner of disinformation against the 1619 Project has been passed to neo-bigots who are expanding its impact on education in schools and businesses. I am incredulous as I watch proud Americans embrace such an assault upon the First Amendment of the United States Constitution. There are those that may not like the way it is being shoved down everyone's throat but are afraid of retaliation by the ones that are in power.

Ms. Jones, I would like to commend you for being there for us. Your words will be immortalized in history because they are too powerful for hatred to erase. There are others who contribute to the pushback against these super bigots, and we may mention some of them later. Those who have the heart to resist a slave's mentality can rest assured that I know your spirit of freedom. I can identify with your urgency and anxiety—the quickening of the desire to correct the course of liberty, lest this vessel stray into unforgiving waters and perhaps sail off to the end of our freedom.

Chapter Five:
The Tenant Farmer

The life of a black tenant farmer was just a little above slavery. The agreement was the tenant farmer would live on a farm in a shack provided by the plantation owner. While living there, he virtually belonged to the plantation owner.

Each house on the plantation had a tin roof painted red. They were built with pine clapboards, which became petrified and took on a dull grayish hue over time. Sometimes the cow pasture would be close to the tenant's house. It was not meant to be cosmopolitan in its appearance.

The tenant farmer was subject to the conditions and rules therein. Those conditions most always meant that your family, including children that were old enough, would work when commanded to work, regardless of what day or hour they were prompted to. Every White man was a boss—even if he was also a tenant farmer. I visited with some friends on a Sunday afternoon and observed the boss telling them that he wanted them to get on the back of the pickup truck that he was driving because he had farm work for them to do. They would have to obey him even though they were not dressed in work garb when he happened to come around.

Some of the plantations had cruel owners who had a reputation for beating their tenants for various reasons. An example: if you claimed sickness as a reason to not work, a straw boss, aka overseer, would beat you. Sometimes the person who was doing the beating would be a Black man. Malcolm X had a name for this person that sounded something like "mouse rigger."

Most times there was a cattle truck that collected the tenants each day and hauled them to the worksite. From sunup to sundown, they would toil in the fields for meager wages. There was an aluminum dipper that every one of the tenants drank water from while working. The water that they consumed came from a stream nearby. I would be the designated water boy and would always get a stern warning to knock the wiggle-tails (mosquito larvae) back.

The same cattle truck mentioned earlier was used to haul some tenants into town on Saturdays to shop. If you somehow were not on that truck when it returned to the plantation, then you had a beating coming.

The gate to the plantation was locked at a designated time on Saturday evenings, and some plantations had a church for their tenants. Our family was fortunate to own our property, but we worked on the farm alongside the farm tenants. We had the option of not working on a farm where the tenants were treated harshly.

The 1900s were tenant farm years for many Black people, but a great migration to Northern states occurred as families packed their meager belongings and stole away under the cover of darkness. I sometimes wondered if they had left the farm and become victims of the ghetto slums with their rat-infested environment. Someone said that every form of refuge has its price.

The 1900s were staunch Jim Crow years. Voting rights for Black people were out of the question until the Voting Rights Act was passed. When the farm tenants went into town, there were separate movie theaters and sections of town that were off limits to them. If a farmhand, as they were called, was jailed, their boss would get them out in time to go to work on Monday morning. It was a sad existence in a world where aspirations were as jailed as the farmhand that got locked up.

Moonshine was the intoxicant that some men used to forget that they were living a life of which they were ashamed, bound by old Jim Crow to a subservient position. The sheriff was the distributor of the moonshine, and he was the epitome of the big-belly, mean Southern sheriff. He arrested a young Black soldier because the soldier objected to being called a boy. This was full-grown Jim Crow stuff.

The entertainment out in the country usually was a juke joint, of which my family had a proprietorship.

I learned the early blues artists' music from the jukebox. The songs told the whole story within their painful lyrics and heartfelt intonations. Today, they bring the tenant farm memories to a stark, nostalgic forefront. We have voting rights in the year 2023, but we don't have the cohesion that we had in the 1900s.

I am relieved that conditions have improved for those that were living on the farm, although there is an emptiness and longing for the closeness that we shared due to being oppressed together.

The older ones are gone, and they took a lot of valuable survival skills with them. They canned food, made quilts, and knew the art of farming for survival. They would aways say that "we have got to press on," which means to persevere against this hatred and exploitation that we endure.

I sometimes have this recurring dream of visiting a warehouse that's filled with old farm equipment. There is a service elevator there, and I take it to the top floor. When I step out of the elevator, it is onto a road that I remember from the old plantation. The old plantation owners are also gone, and their young ones are building mansions with the profits made from the strong backs of the Black tenant farmers. If there is a silver lining to this drama, it is that we have an educated young group that can navigate through the legal system. They are the children and grandchildren of tenant farmers. If I could give them one small piece of advice, it would be to "press on."

Chapter Six:
The Federal, State, and
Local Court Systems

In this chapter I intend to examine the federal courts and what impact they have on our quality of life. I am starting with the federal court system because the United States Constitution holds the key to our civil rights.

The United States District Court is the lowest federal court. If a federal law has been broken or a civil suit is filed against a party, it must start in a district court that has the proper jurisdiction to hear the case. An example of a case where the federal court may have jurisdiction to handle a civil suit is an infringement upon someone's patent or civil rights under the applicable laws. At the present time, a case against the Florida "woke law" has been filed in federal court. This law has been blocked temporarily.

The second level of federal courts is the United States Circuit Court of Appeals. At this level of the federal court system, a plaintiff or the defendant may file an appeal if they are dissatisfied with the results of the United States District Court's proceedings. Courts of Appeals can set precedents with their rulings for other cases, which, when used, are called case law.

The Fifth Circuit Court of Appeals has jurisdiction over Mississippi, Texas, and Louisiana. It recently upheld a Mississippi Jim Crow era voting restriction law that was instituted in 1890 to disenfranchise Black voters but was amended in 1968. The majority and the dissenting justices confirmed that the law was designed to keep Black people from voting. The majority opinion found that because the law had been amended in 1968, the original intent of denying voting rights to Black voters was no longer held. The amended version was declared to be reenacted but in effect was an amended version of the same racist law. This ruling will be appealed to the United States Supreme Court.

The United States Supreme Court is the highest court in the court system. There we have nine justices. They can hear cases from the lower courts at their discretion.

The fate of Roe v. Wade was determined in the SCO-TUS. The jurors (justices) are trusted to be apolitical, meaning they are ruling without the influence of a political party. A look at the rulings is a telling indication of the political party that has benefited.

The cases that pertain to each level of the federal court system, such as the Florida "antiwoke law," have to do with constitutional rights. The Florida "antiwoke law" seems to target the African American specifically in its intent to stifle the First Amendment rights of free speech. This is evident by the banning of critical race theory and the 1619 Project in our schools. Any attempt at fairness for Black people is met with admonishing results—as when the attempt was made to recruit a Black hockey player. A judge mentioned the "dystopian" aspect of the "woke law," which describes a society where suffering and mistreatment of the inhabitants is prevalent.

The overturning of Roe v. Wade by the United States Supreme Court dealt a tremendous setback to women's right to choose to have an abortion. Cases like this one are instituted by right-wing conservatives. Six of the nine Justices on the United States Supreme Court were appointed by right-wing conservative presidents. Their rulings have favored those political ideologies. Federal judges are appointed for life.

To understand the federal court system in America, one must understand the power of the organization that influences the nomination of judges. The Federalist Society is influential in the choice of federal judges. They have a pool of conservative judges that are sympathetic to their right-wing ideologies. From this pool they have offered conservative judges Clarence Thomas, Neil Gorsuch, Amy Comey Barrett, Brett Cavanaugh, Chief Justice John Roberts, and Samuel Alito—the architect of the demise of Roe v. Wade.

The Federalist Society was formed by a small group of college students. The organization has grown to become a "movement," as it was described by its president Leonard Leo. It is well funded by deep pockets of dark money, from which a current political candidate for the Republican presidency can also benefit to advance their far-right agendas. They are effectively buying the power of the courts, and this has cast a shadow upon our constitutional rights.

The Supreme Court of Florida is the highest state court in the State of Florida. The County Courts are the lowest courts in Florida's court system. The state supreme court has seven judges—the chief justice and six justices who are appointed by the governor to six-year terms. It is the final step in Florida's court system—above all courts in the State of Florida. The District Court of Appeals is the intermediate institution under the Supreme Court of Florida. There are six district courts of appeals. A step lower are twenty circuit courts, which are state courts and trial courts of the original jurisdiction. The county courts have original jurisdiction over county misdemeanors and civil cases under $30,000.

The state courts have far more jurisdiction than the federal courts—they handle cases of criminal as well as civil disputes and cases involving breaches of contracts.

The powerful state attorney, also called the district attorney, is the top prosecutor in a given judicial circuit. Under American law, government prosecuting attorneys have nearly absolute and unreviewable power to choose whether to bring criminal charges and what charges to bring. This power is accorded so that plea-bargaining and flexibility in the process are advantageous to the prosecutor.

In the political atmosphere of 1963 Alabama, prosecutors declined to bring charges against the Klansmen who murdered four young Black girls in a Birmingham church, even though they were identified by the FBI. Further, records show that federal investigators have brought cases to prosecution involving infractions by southern Whites against Black people, yet these cases were not prosecuted by state attorneys on a frequent basis. Political pressure from Jim Crow groups has frightened prosecutors into caring more about being reelected than the desire to prosecute old Jim Crow. They also could, in some cases, be part of an extremist group.

The Bureau of Prisons states that Blacks are far more likely to be stopped, searched, arrested, and sentenced to prison than their White counterparts. The power invested in state attorneys results in Blacks being incarcerated at five times the rate of Whites. Relatedly, the National Registry of Exoneration finds that innocent Black people are nineteen times more likely to be convicted of drug crimes than innocent Whites—a much larger disparity than we see for murder and rape—even though White and Black Americans use illegal drugs at a similar rate.

There are more cases and studies that support racial disparities in the court systems, and I will visit these Jim Crow injustices later. The weight of oppression that I have written about in this book leaves no doubt that we are fighting an uphill struggle to remain alive in these United States. There have been martyrs and champions in our struggles. And while we are examining the court system, there are two opposing court justices that I would like to write about.

The Honorable Thurgood Marshall was a real hero, to me and to his people. There are cases to prove his worth. Most notable to me is Brown v. Board of Education. He championed civil rights for all people and was appointed to the United States Court of Appeals by President John F. Kennedy. In 1965 President Lyndon Johnson appointed him to the post of Solicitor General—someone who argues cases for the United States Government before the United States Supreme Court.

In 1967 he was appointed to the Supreme Court. This appointment was vigorously opposed by the Republicans, but he was seated as the first Black justice on the high court. He became very fond of the United States Constitution after having to recite it in school when he was six years old. He was especially fond of the Bill of Rights.

From government archives, we know that the first ten amendments to the constitution form the Bill of Rights. It spells out Americans' rights under the government. Regardless of how many "woke" laws are Jim-Crowed out of Florida, the Bill of Rights guarantees civil rights and liberties to the individual—including freedom of speech, press, and religion. It sets rules for due process of law and reserves all powers not delegated to the Federal Government to the people of the states. It specifies that "the enumeration in the Constitution, of certain rights shall not be construed to <u>deny</u> or <u>disparage</u> others retained by the people" (emphasis added). I think that this language challenges the textualist concept that the supermajority in SCO-TUS is using to disparage some plaintiffs. This is the work that Justice Thurgood Marshall dedicated his life to. He was a great champion of civil rights.

The Republicans chose the next Black justice to serve on the high court. He was nominated by President George H. W. Bush to the court after Justice Thurgood Marshall retired. The Republicans must have had a good laugh at this maneuver. Today he is recognized as the most conservative justice on the Supreme court. The mention of his name brings negative comments from people who are struggling to survive in a society that is going after our rights with a political hatchet. His worldview was shaped by conservative authors at Yale University, which is home to the Heritage Foundation.

I can visualize the indoctrination with subtle dialogue: "You're smarter than those other boys. You shouldn't be wasting your time on subjects that no one likes or even gives a damn about. You should be in the business of helping to shape the direction of this country. You are a perfect fit in our society."

My assessment of this tragedy is reminiscent of a character played by Samuel L. Jackson in the movie *Django*. The character was meaner to his people than the slave master. When a Black man can out-Crow Old Jim Crow, I am perplexed with confusion.

To have a foundation built upon <u>textualism,</u> the concept of which is to interpret the Constitution exactly as the slave-owning Founding Fathers originally intended, would have you somewhere on a slave plantation. The Fourteenth Amendment brought the first law to establish a court case for freedom for Black people. Again, "the enumeration of rights spelled out in the Constitution shall not be construed to deny or disparage others retained by the people." SCOTUS should adhere to this principle.

The first part of the court system that most Black people encounter in their neighborhoods daily is law enforcement. They are the enforcement arm of the ironclad Jim Crow network. They may have a bone to pick as well. The following is an example.

THEY KILLED JAMES BRAZIER. On April 20, 1958, James Brazier, the African American victim, was arrested by Dawson Police Department officers Weyman Cherry and Randolph McDonald and charged with interfering with the arrest of his father. James had already been arrested seven times by Weyman Cherry, who had commented on the fact that James had always been able to buy a new car and called him a smart son of a b——.

As a result of the interference with the arresting of James's father, Weyman Cherry came to James's house and beat him unmercifully with a "blackjack." James was then arrested and taken to jail. The attending physician stated that James smelled of alcohol and was probably drunk. He was locked up in the women's ward and placed on notice to be awakened every two hours. Finally, he was taken to a hospital, where he was found to have a fractured skull. He died two days later.

Weyman Cherry was promoted to chief of police.

Chapter Seven:
The Legislature

A look at the House of Representatives in 2023 is scary. At present they are trying to reinstall the forty-fifth administration of the office of president of the United States. Can this be real? The Republican-controlled House is ignoring the infamous January 6 attack on the Capitol Building, where the business of tallying the electoral votes was in process. The forty-fifth president put his vice president's life in jeopardy and called him a coward and worse for not throwing the election. With the GOP holding a slim majority in the House, the Republicans are saying that it's OK to overthrow the government and reinstall Mr. Bigotry.

The forty-fifth president has just been indicted by a grand jury, with charges brought forth by a Black prosecutor from New York. This is causing a great deal of hellraising by right-wing Republicans, and I suspect there are a lot more people who are being quiet. My mind is leaning toward the dialogue "How dare you— who are not even a White man—attempt to arrest our greatest Viking? We may throw you a bone sometimes, and now you want to arrest *your* master?" Remember what was written in an earlier chapter: "It isn't against the law if it is against a Black person." I hear them saying, "Someone needs to talk to this boy."

The nation is holding its breath. I am reading the language around people who are devout conservatives. There are whispers of stepping up racist actions against Black citizens, including meting out harsher court sentences and doubling down on stop, search, and seizure by policemen. A ludicrous thought to me, and yet a statement was made some time ago by the forty-fifth president that he could pardon himself. If that is possible, then why would he respond to any charge of a crime? A United States president can't pardon state crimes.

So maybe the timing is off just a little for the Black prosecutor because this would-be fascist may cancel the other would-be fascists, or vice versa. We are not amazed, for the image of Rosewood still burns in our memories after one hundred years. We must be diligent in our intelligence-gathering and exercise our gifts of discernment. We must monitor the animosity that could boil over at this time. The herd mentality will override fake friendship—and no, we can't all become "Blacks for Trump." MAGA MEANS JIM CROW!

The United States Congress is made up of two chambers. The upper chamber is the Senate, and the lower chamber is the House of Representatives. At present, the House Republicans are in control of the lower chamber, while the Senate has a Democratic majority. When working in unison, they have the power to check the Supreme Court. Congress can legislate laws or amend statutes to overturn Supreme Court decisions. To overturn a Constitutional interpretation is more complex because Article Five of the US Constitution allows Congress to amend the Constitution by two-thirds vote of both houses and two-thirds of the states, if requested. I can't envision any decision short of activating the NORAD missile system that would bring these two parties to an agreement at this time.

We have a perfect storm brewing that starts with Jim Crow governors feeding racist laws through their state legislatures, with nods from a supermajority, non-apolitical Supreme Court, and a willing majority of US representatives who are also ultraconservatives. The district courts have intervened to check some of these Jim Crow laws on occasion, but appeals courts such as the Fifth Circuit Court of Appeals have upheld such bogus hate laws, as was mentioned earlier. The idea of expanding the Supreme Court hasn't been mentioned lately. What can be done? Vote—it's still legal!

There is power held by the people that can change the quality of life for us citizens. We can vote our way out of a coming disaster. We can't wait for someone else to do it for us. Wishing and wanting is not getting it done. If we don't vote, someone else will place a dictator into power. We will be the losers.

There are states that would deny a voter a drink of water on a hot day. There are states that have used identification credentials to prevent citizens from voting. Drop boxes have been removed, and shorter voting periods have been used to suppress voter turnout. If it is important enough to go to these great lengths, the voter should make a concerted effort to overcome these obstacles. Voting means that my constituents can see that I am trustworthy. I believe that a person who won't vote is stealing a free ride. I would not leave my fellow soldier to fight our struggle alone.

The House Republicans have established a subcommittee against weaponization of the Federal Government! It's true, the Republican majority has a faction that is designed to investigate government officials who investigate far-right Republicans. This is the platform they are standing on. If the committee can go after prosecutors and dismantle their case against an indicted person, we are all in trouble. It will mean that there is no law for would-be dictators, regardless of how many laws those people break.

The nation is waiting for the judge to rule on the suit filed against the subcommittee chair because of his intent to obstruct a legal proceeding. The audacious campaign to malign the New York prosecutor is led by the same people that spoke so forcefully during the forty-fifth president's impeachment hearings. They are painting a picture of gloom and doom.

The head of Homeland Security is heaping praise upon Air National Guardsman Jack Teixeira and has stated that the President is the real enemy. She said that the traitor is White, male, Christian, and anti-war. It may seem to be a cute political stunt, but it is a depiction of the low-class position that the leaders of the House of Representatives have sunk into. Racist innuendoes are now being substituted for the lack of conscientious programs that can serve the nation's citizens. Morons only have moronic ideas, as when she came up with the brilliant idea of dividing the nation into red and blue states. Dignity and grace are conspicuously absent from this program. This is the congress-woman who illegally infringed upon someone's copy-righted material. She then resorted to racial epithets and labeled him a drug addict. This is the low-class, self-serving behavior of the second-in-command under the house majority leader.

Chapter Eight:
Alexandria and the
Glorious Years

———————◆———————

There was a time in history when an empire on the African continent was rich and powerful. Alexandria was a beacon of prosperity where people from abroad could visit and enjoy the vast intellectual fruits of its university. It is time to revisit the culture from whence we come.

Did Aristotle plagiarize philosophy from ancient Egypt? I will attempt to approach this controversial topic with great respect—not only because scholars on one side of the issue find it extremely important to establish an un-African history of the contribution to medicine, law, and philosophy from Africa to the Western world, but also because on the other side of the issue is an adamant argument that the Greeks stole the treasures from ancient Africa.

Mary Lefkowitz, in her book *Not Out of Africa*, gives compelling evidence that Greece's independent contributions are divorced from an inheritance of Egyptian culture. Lower Egypt at the time of Alexandria's prominence was truly African in indigenous culture and humanity. I have looked closely at her work to find evidence that the contributions from Greece were not of African origin. The hot topic of philosophy being stolen from Egypt is foremost among the concepts to be disproved or proved. The reviews are numerous and competitive. There are reviews that even question the African people's indigenous presence in Egypt, due to the physical appearance of Egyptians today. I have also noted that natives of Timbuktu do look to be African today. Where's the beginning?

I will start with a question. Why is the debate centered around the glory of Alexandria? Modern-day scholars make scant mention of the important city of Rhacotis that thrived in ancient Egypt on the northern coast. This city was renamed Alexandria after the arrival of Alexander the Great. The so-called culture war's label, which describes twenty-first-century full-blown racism being resisted by African Americans, is a player in this drama. Scholars on both sides of the struggle are searching for the truth, with some not-so-hidden agendas in the mix. I shall apply the label Afrocentric to scholars striving to maintain who they truly are, against the misinformed opinions of Eurocentrics who may be contradicting their own forthright convictions based on the calculations of time periods to disprove the intellectual comprehension by Greeks from 900 to 300 BCE of the Egyptian dialect. This is now being disputed with twenty-first-century misinformation that dismisses their (the Greeks) claims as "fake news." The Greeks in question are supporting the Africans' importance to Western philosophy! Modern scholars of the Western nations claim that the Greeks could not comprehend the Egyptian dialect and thus were unable to support the contributions made by the Egyptians (Africans). We then must be wary of Eurocentric practices of undervaluing non-European societies as inferior to Western ones. This undervaluing is especially practiced against Asians and Africans in the ideological context of "I came, I saw, I conquered" to promote imminent domain and Western superiority.

My curiosity compels me to accept Alexandria as a hub of great importance with people from all cultures doing business with the indigenous inhabitants before Alexander the Great, but why would only the Greeks have trouble with communication? That theory makes it convenient for Aristotle to set up shop in Alexandria after the downfall of the indigenous people of the region. But there is more.

Alexandria was named in 331 BCE by Alexander the Great. This was at least nine to ten years before the death of Aristotle in 322 BCE. The countdown would add years to Aristotle's life. Thus Aristotle certainly had time to obtain African artifacts from Egypt before the invasion and subsequent downfall of Rhacotis. Mary Lefkowitz's calculations are in error as she tries to prove that Alexandria was not established before Aristotle's death. Some scholars claim that Aristotle never visited Egypt, and there are scholars that have Aristotle spending twenty years advancing his education in Egypt before the invasion of Egypt by Alexander the Great in 332 BCE, when Aristotle got the opportunity to ransack leading Egyptian libraries. It was said that from there he went to Peripatetic and founded his academy in Athens. If Aristotle did not steal from Alexandria, it doesn't exonerate his theft of Egyptian philosophy, which existed long before the existence of Alexandria. This fact is proven by the very first civilization in lower Egypt, which established the Empire of Kemet.

The Kemetians built a civilization before any other nation in history. Indeed, the root of modern civilization goes back to ancient Egyptian civilization. This fact has been ignored for some reason. The Kemetians advanced the study of ancient Egyptian philosophy. Egyptian culture had great influence on Western civilization as well as on the Indian population Dradidian. From the moment the Greek philosophers stepped onto the soil of Africa, especially Kemet, to study Egyptian spiritual teachings from 900 to 300 BCE, Western culture radically changed. Therefore, it is necessary for seekers of the truth to study the culture of ancient Egypt and its cultural heritage.

Kemet, which was the part of ancient Egypt in the Nile Basin of northeast Africa, constructed a civilization dating back to the year 5500 BCE. This civilization thrived until the year 30 BCE, when the Roman leader Octavius (Augustus) won the last Kingdom of Ptolemaic, which was ruled by Queen Cleopatra. It was then declared a Roman state. There were many invaders of Ancient Egypt, but the culture influenced all who came.

Ancient Egyptians referred to their homeland as Kemet State. According to historian Anta Diop, the Egyptians referred to themselves as "Black" people of KMT, and KM was the etymological root of other words such as KAM or HAM, which refer to Black people in the Hebrew tradition.

While acknowledging that Egypt was invaded by different nations, with Timbuktu understood to have been subject to the French invasion, I maintain that these invaders were influenced by the great civilization of ancient Kemet, whose culture founded the philosophical basis of Western culture. When most people think of ancient Egyptian civilization, their minds go to the age of the families ruled by a series of kings divided into families and the late period of the family age, 2100 to about 1000 BCE, the period in which the Old Testament influenced Israeli Christian culture. The history of the Sphinx dates to much older times than the Egyptian scientists assume; the latest archaeological evidence dates it to 10,000 BCE due to traces of water that evince its existence during the rainy age. Kemet is still alive because of its culture.

Chapter Nine:
Redemption

The cavalry has arrived to save the European historians from the notion that mere Black-skinned so-called myth seekers are in their midst—claiming knowledge of themselves over the knowledge of those privileging Eurocentric values. They may be assuming—or may be insinuating—that a black smudge was found in the records and the history of Egypt had to be sanitized because the whole of Western culture was threatened with being compromised. Therefore, the justification of oppression against our unbridled free expression is no longer on trial.

Baldwin sought to mitigate the European weakness that has compelled them to join the bandwagon of tradition, where even lynchings can be normalized. I understand the tradition but can't understand the two-headed decision to commit mass genocide because that's just the way it is. My understanding may be clouded by the echoes of the millions of screams from innocent victims who have dared to sample the sweetness of freedom outside of a slave ship. An attempt to have a bluegrass conversation with sympathetic overtones would be seen by me as asking to understand the predicament that places them in a position of fearing me, based on forces that require them to believe a "birther theory," thereby placing a stamp of disapproval on my future. I know this to be true because they abruptly disavow me in every manner of lies, gestures, and body language when one of their peers suddenly approaches without notice while we are engaging in normal conversations. It is very hard to believe a lie no matter how skillful the liar.

We have the culture of decency from our Kemetian ancestors, lifting us up with their political and economic values based on spirituality, thus establishing an organized society based on the principle of racial equality and founded on a judicial experience inspired by cosmic laws and seeking to make the world on Earth a picture of the heavenly world. It lifts my self-esteem, in a nation where superhighways of failure are constructed to carry me on a journey to nowhere. Marcus Garvey dared to envision a place like Kemet—a place devoid of racist cops, lurking on back roads in wait for their hapless prey. A place where a tremendous amount of energy is conserved, not burned in a mental and emotional state of mind from the rigors of running toward freedom, never quite crossing the goal line, yet running until the gas tank is empty, then passing the baton to another runner who is already running toward the same goal line, and so forth and so on…

There is a reckoning to be had. We descendants of slaves need not fear that we are committing a sin when we breathe deeply the fresh thoughts of independent creativity. We can construct our universe in an isolated region within the private recesses of our minds. There we can have an uninterrupted approach to our economic welfare—and these plans must be confidential and top secret, only for our eyes, lest they be snatched from us and stomped to death as was Mary Turner's unborn child, in a lynching not far from here. The snatchers of our dreams are the same haters who labeled us unworthy to fly out of Tuskegee and into the Third Reich with a skill that stirred the desire of haters to go out and lynch a thousand Kemetian babies using Herod's method of preventing kings from advancing. These personal and private treasures that we reward ourselves with within our minds may be the therapy that prevents our stooping to the level of cruelty that we endure, but our babies may be confused.

There being no tenant farms to escape from, the children of the tenant farmers were as far north as possible, given the meager clothes and food one might find in the ghetto. The dream of a big-belly sheriff leading a mob of angry lynchers gave way to the reality of rat-infested high-rise slums, where the babies are ill prepared to find the safety that their parents sought by migrating north. This is, after all, still America, where their foreparents arrived in chains on a ship—as property of big business, which is no stranger to the merchants of New York City. So it is a reality that from sea to shining sea, there is a special hell for African Americans that is common to the region of hell. No one is there to tell the babies to "press on" against the entrapment of a ghetto prison, where the only way out is death. Scant food laden with unhealthy additives—coupled with contaminated water, with a dose of air pollution more deadly than the shotgun of a Southern sheriff—is a daily normalcy in the ghetto. Someone is capitalizing on the predicaments, because guns and drugs and liquor stores are plentiful. There being no respite but the beckoning call from the community church, the lost child seeks a haven behind the heavy doors of the godly sanctuary only to find (in too many instances) that the father is a monster hiding behind a mask of holiness, and this is but another trap laid for an innocent child to be molested. This then being the box canyon of existence for the child, he makes a desperate decision to use the gun and drugs to work his way out of a hopeless conundrum.

This song and dance are played out in other scenarios, as when the child goes to a school and kills innocent schoolchildren, but this time because they are unable to separate hypocrisy from reality. The truth today must be the truth tomorrow also, lest young minds become confused and say, "You know what, I will fix it." They are following the examples set by their parents. If the parents have a history of murder—as in the "The Waco Horror"—the child believes that it is OK to do so. The parents didn't fully explain that it was only minorities who were to be killed. Wasn't the West conquered by murdering the Indians? It's right there on television, big as day. The "alternative truth" is I am politically incorrect. I should say simply that the West was won. The reality is I don't stand on political correctness or any other whitewashing of critical race theory.

The reality is Americans turn up the rhetoric on the horrors of Auschwitz, which was a place of mass genocide, while keeping silent on the horrors of the millions lost in the Atlantic and in the cotton fields of America.

There was a concerto played at Khe-Sahn, Vietnam. Those who were there told the reality of the marines being pinned down for forty-nine days by the enemy. It was called the "Forty-Nine Days of Khe-Sahn." The mortar rounds that fell caused the clay to color everyone the same. This made them as close to blood brothers as was possible. They depended on and trusted each other. The reality is your buddy from Khe-Sahn might deny you three thousand times while standing alongside Jim Crow.

Securely tucked into a blanket that is labeled "made in America," we bed down for the night—Jim Crow and us—secure that we can find enough cohesion for our common welfare, for we are now part of the fabric, each in our respective ideologies, that binds this nation together. We who are struggling to become somewhat more than a silent partner have wet our beaks in the heady wine of hypocrisy—sometimes as commanded and at other times to earn a seat finally at Jim Crow's table. Either way we remain complicit for we had a role in the downfall of the Indians. Once they are seated at the table, there are those who commanded and wielded power—such as the buffalo soldiers, whom the Indians named because of their hair, like the fur of a buffalo, and because they were fierce soldiers in battle—and then there are those who are like a slave cylinder that is in a fixed position and can only travel in one direction, and then only when pressure is applied. This one is likened to a court jester who, as all can see, is the world's greatest fool but a valuable "willing fool."

The 1960s saw me coming of age to be of service to America. I left home and went to the US Army by selective service in 1965. I was in Vietnam from 1966 to 1967. I was too naïve and country to smoke marijuana or get hooked on drugs in Southeast Asia. Many soldiers came back with a drug addiction. When I came home, it was to the "Age of Aquarius." The people my age wore long hair and Afros, and flower child attitudes were in vogue. White guys were calling black guys "brother," and vice versa. I marveled at this turn of events and rejoiced at this change of heart. They even smoked a joint together, which was unthinkable just a few years earlier. It was a far cry from the tenant farm existence, because this time everyone smoked from the same weed instead of drinking from the same dipper. The civil rights movement was in fifth gear, and the gay rights movement rode its coattails into freedom. It must have scared the hell out of Jim Crow for a minute, but he came roaring back with a vengeance.

By then we had gotten into the groove with a song from Funkadelic called "Free Your Mind…and Your Ass Will Follow." Curtis Mayfield welcomed us "Back to the World." Black lights adorned crash pads with posters that invited you into the world of Doofus Drake. The world certainly was more congenial, what with civil rights leaders such as Eldridge Cleaver, Stokely Carmichael, the Black Panthers, and Rev. Dr. Martin Luther King Jr. at the forefront of the movement.

It was in the late 1960s that Jim Crow started killing people in a move that, to me, seemed to strike at the heart of the movement. Big names such as Senator Robert F. Kennedy, Dr. Martin Luther King, and the Black Panthers fell like dominoes. President Lyndon Johnson did not seek a second term. White folks would still share a joint, but the brother "hypocrisy" was fading. I still felt as if there had been a redemption of sorts—a respite from the kick-ass world of the 1950s. I also knew that our attitudes would never be the same. After all, we still had Baldwin to keep us looking at what we should be aspiring to.

Now we are in the year 2023, and the far-right Republicans have just voted against adding an equal rights amendment to the United States Constitution. This is hardball racism with an in-your-face attitude. Dutifully, the slave cylinder pistoned his vote against his own freedom as was commanded by Jim Crow, and it added more weight to the wagon of oppression.

Chapter Ten:
The Gadfly Syndrome

Scientists have used numerous methods in a relentless push to determine the intelligence of a race of people. The search takes us back to ancient Egypt and the earliest civilizations. The question of a Black race being established in Lower Egypt is undisputable, but the concept of intellect is why every stone has been overturned to find a flaw in the race. Scholars have different opinions about the racial makeup of the early Egyptians.

In the eighteenth and early nineteenth centuries, scholars adopted the concepts of racial hierarchy using craniometry and anthropometry systems. Some scholars argued that ancient Egyptians culture was influenced by the introduction of Asian-language-speaking people who supposedly brought a higher intelligence to Egypt after the races were mixed. Their claim is of a superior race called Afroasiatic from the mix. Others point to Nubian groups or populations from Europe as being influential in the intellectual advances of the ancient Egyptians. These hypotheses were based on the science of using the shape of an individual's skull (craniology) to determine their intelligence. I see football linebackers with heads that I can believe have been reshaped by using them as battering rams.

Seriously, the Kemetians needed no introduction from another race to build a culturally sound empire. Despite multiple foreign invasions, the demographics remained largely intact. I think that the moral of this story is again the Eurocentric ideology being aggressive in the quest for dominance. The gadfly syndrome comes into play when the status quo of the races is disturbed enough that it compels the scholars to hunt for something to prove that they are the masters of the universe—as a junkie will roam the streets until he gets that all-powerful fix that his system is craving for, will even kill for. The Europeans should not feel that their humanity is compromised unless they bring about the destruction of ours. As I stated earlier, we all have wet our beaks in the heady wine of this nation's successes and failures, so there is no reason to torment us relentlessly as a gadfly might antagonize its victims. We remain un-dehumanized. We are here. We are here until some mad person finds a way to launch the birds at NORAD or some other country launches theirs. With millions of starving babies, intelligent cultures are ignoring, with nonchalant arrogance, the pitiful little children and are spending trillions on ways to destroy mankind. Maybe someone should see if their head is shaped intelligently.

Extremists are thirsting for mass genocide using "replacement theory" as an excuse. The national election came too soon, and far-right conservatives have proven that they are willing to sabotage the process for the sake of placing an extremist in the White House. If the midterms seemed scary, we now have laws being legislated against our race with willing legislators and fascist-oriented governors. I hate to disturb the peace, but there is a snake in the grass, and I am alarmed that not enough people are concerned about the direction in which we are headed.

"The caste system," as examined by Ms. Isabel Wilkerson, offers a stark view of the clamoring for hierarchy. King Solomon coined the phrase "What profits the wise man over the fool, or the rich man over the poor?" It may be that the Christian White nationalists are reading from a different text. The gadfly is busy, as the Christian faith is the flag being flown during the march toward the cause of pure White nationalism. This effort toward supremacy supports Ms. Wilkerson's assertion of the caste system is that it excludes people from wealth by using the color of their skin as a marker. I salute you, Isabel Wilkerson, for your contribution to the wokeness that you have shared with us.

Willie Lynch also mentioned skin color as a method to control the slaves by the slave owner. The sight of a Black person with wealth is reason to ridicule and label them with false innuendos such as "they must be selling drugs." This label may mean that if they have a job that pays that well, then one of us is being short-changed. This is not all Europeans' philosophy because Jim Crow will not deplete his coffers for an ideology. This is evidenced by the many homeless white people in America. However, appearances availeth much in the caste system, and so does the hypocrisy of the White supremacy ideology. Therefore, lies are being told of how other races are the reason for economic woes and poverty in the White community. The political gadfly never sleeps. We should be clever and "woke" to the guiles of the ones who are coming as thieves, intending to destroy us. My warnings are throughout this writing.

Cities that have Black mayors are the ones where so-called illegal immigrants are being shipped. The far-right

House Republicans are holding federal social programs such as veterans benefits and Social Security benefits as ransom against food stamps and the like, as a bargaining chip in the federal debt ceiling hike. The poorest citizens are again threatened by the right-wing super bigots. Big fat bigots who have not paid their way and are riding on the backs of the working class are stirring the same old cauldron of discord that they have used as a wedge against inclusion and diversity for decades. Deep pockets are paving the road to financial hell, on which unwary travelers are treading regardless of race, creed, color, and some religions. Ridiculous crusades (Walt Disney World) are launched against legitimate businesses without regard for their constitutional rights. This seems to me to be a giant red herring to cover something more sinister (authoritarian government), or it is one of the greatest fool's errands in the history of America? Therefore, be wary, for the bigots have begun to brag again.

The following cliches serve to describe the state of treachery that I perceive within the far-right political system. "There is no honor among thieves," if you remember. "Every goodbye isn't gone, and every shut eye isn't asleep." The beat goes on to the drumbeat of the movement that manufactured the January 6 insurrection. Sedition at this point would be the straw that breaks this Democratic camel's back, and our vessel of hope, which sails upon the sea of our freedom, will list precariously to starboard, or even take on enough bigotry to sink.

Some states, such as Mississippi and Florida, are muscling in on local governments peremptorily with state police—using the excuse of controlling crime. How much control will they exert before we are living in a police state? If you add the subcommittee created by the far-right House Republicans to investigate legitimate law enforcement entities, a plot begins to sprout. He who has brains, let him think. We are so comfortable in our luxurious lives that we can't fathom the reality of what's going on in our nation. All the above anomalies are happening in the United States.

Someone said that after committing all manner of infractions against the nation and against its people, the super bigot is picking up steam in his quest for the US presidency. The table is being set! The hate-mongers are marching along with the Christians! It looks as if the wolves have joined the sheep in a kind of brotherhood! The question that is before us is: how much of this circus is a political vote-getting stunt, and how much of it is an authoritarian expedition? Beware! Jim Crow is lurking in the midst.

We of the African American race are just one component in this mixed bag of humanity that is the makeup of America. Our roots are planted here now. We know this system because we have died for it. We need that same dedication for our survival. So ponder the evidence. States are sending an overload of so-called illegal immigrants to cities with Black mayors, as I have mentioned. State governors are using rubber-stamp state legislators to pass bogus White nationalist laws, and state laws are being legislated to remove from office prosecutors that refuse to prosecute people who defy these bogus laws. States are creating police forces that are taking over cities with the pretext of preventing crime. This is a concerted effort, which means that there is a master plan against African Americans that has already been thought out. Again, we are neither mute nor amazed! This time Jim Crow is going full throttle!

It is no misstep that anyone can now own and carry a gun—whether blind, crippled, or crazy. The plot could thicken into a backlash from veterans and government workers with outcries of social programs given to those lazy N-words.

There is an obscure provision in the Fourteenth Amendment to the United States Constitution that gives the President the power to continue meeting the financial obligations of the government as needed. This is on an emergency basis. Republicans complain about government spending when the spending doesn't favor their rich constituents. Poor people are confused by the inflationary situation at the grocery stores and what are called kitchen table items. The rich folks own the grocery stores and can gouge the poor folks' paychecks with high prices. These situations then are blamed on Democratic administrations in a ruse to change administrations at the next election.

Black people understand these games that Republicans play, and we understand the ruthless policies that are perpetrated upon us daily. So we have an understanding. We understand as we understood in chapter two on "woke." We understand that there is an evil force with a grip on the American dream—as African Americans struggle to survive. This evil force is <u>hate</u>. Hate is like a filthy rag used to clean the kennels of a thousand hounds of hell. A filthy rag brought into the house as a trophy, not unlike the head of a hapless moose that adorns the wall of a proud hunter. There it rests as a memorial to a dank, damp captain of a four-hundred-year-old slave ship that still sails on an imaginary Atlantic Ocean, with its pitiful cargo of souls who are predestined for centuries of antiwoke laws, and merciless torture from merciless slave owners, and antiwoke lawmakers. It was worth repeating, because of the gadfly-like never-ending oppression that's mounted by Jim Crow.

Our successes are ignored—and our failures are applauded. This is evident in the absence of coverage of our accomplishments in mainstream media, except when we are being prosecuted or else in the context of some similar degrading event. So, although we are estranged partners in this nation and although we pledge allegiance to the same flag, we people of color are like a weak component on a powerful machine that maintains a constantly high rpm while we labor to perform due to neglected maintenance. We must applaud our resilience for stoically marching through four hundred years of hell.

So we march, Jim Crow and us. Strange bedfellows—each with our precious devices of survival, including an independence of each other, yet mechanisms of the same engine called America. Our crying is their laughing, and their crying is karma, we proclaim, but our victories are mere preludes to their vengeances. This brotherhood is one that is wrought with gadflies.

Chapter Eleven:
Summary of the Big Push

W e who are the recipients of oppression endured by our foreparents endeavor to not stoop to the level of cruelty that we endure. This is for the hope of a better life after our death. We bear witness to those who aspire to be presidents while moonlighting as dictators. We bear witness to laws aimed as guns toward our freedom—such as laws against "wokeness." These laws are in direct opposition to our First Amendment rights.

We have traveled down the road of free-for-all-lynchings of our people, as well as the atrocities perpetrated upon the indigenous natives of this land. Concerted efforts have been made by Jim Crow to stifle our youth's attempts to make known the complicity found within our laws—contributing to the complex roadblock to our civil rights, thus compromising our freedom.

Although we endure the oppressed state in which we must navigate our survival, it is our duty as citizens to uphold the responsibilities of citizenship in this country. We must forever "press on" against the "audacity of hate." Don't vote for someone because they can be crueler than the other candidate. Don't vote for a candidate because he looks like a good guy. He may be a slave cylinder. Remember that a slave cylinder is following orders from Jim Crow. Don't forget to research our past as much as possible, for you will be astounded that so many contributions originated with our ancestors in ancient Kemet. Much has been distorted by Eurocentric and Eurasian misinformation.

Press on against the entity that I have labeled as Jim Crow, representing every law that harbors and dispenses hatred toward our people simply for the cause of a White nationalist ideology. An ideology that can only be satisfied when people of color submit to being a kind of subservient fool, and this in totality. History has given us evidence that Jim Crow's nest has been found not only in the molehills of Mississippi but in the hallowed halls of the House of Representatives and the Senate chambers of Congress.

Pay no attention to the losers who may rejoice in my difficult struggle for my uninhibited humanity. They gave their souls without shame to a subservient ideology as if selling that soul would solve the four-hundred-year-old racial problem. I say that those people that choose to not seek the truth of our past must be nurtured and guided toward the truth, for although their bodies may be free, their minds are still in shackles.

Press on because the expected results from SCOTUS cases are now front and center. The affirmative action program has been gutted by the far-right majority, to the surprise of no one. The ripple effect will be made known soon, because businesses will get the nod to discriminate against Black Americans at will. Press on against this Jim Crow thrust to cast us back into his shackles of slavery. Press on against the appointments he has made to the far-right courts, which are anything but apolitical. This result was accomplished with the help of a vast number of conservative donations. The face of the beast against affirmative action is SFFA (Students for Fair Admissions), the bulk of whose funding comes from conservative foundations such as DonorsTrust, the Searle Freedom Trust, the Sarah Scaife Foundation, and the 85 Fund. There are also a multitude of individual Jim Crow donors contributing to the resurrection of slavery by chipping away at the foundations of our freedom. PRESS ON. Again, the culprit behind this big push against African American freedom is Jim Crow, who placed the super majority of jurists on the Supreme Court. I am writing in <u>bold</u> because of the alarming situation that we are confronting and the fact that not enough protest is issuing forth from concerned citizens. A small hole in the dam can flood a city.

Chapter Twelve: Summary Continued, Smiling Faces

That buddy that you thought you knew turned out to be someone who was just trying to gain your confidence. He will use that as a leg up. He will expose whatever secrets you convey to him, and he will make it seem as if he outsmarted you to get them. I know of a slave cylinder who married Jim Crow. This is a classic example of someone who wanted the world to think that he was just that big of a fool, but the truth is he is an even bigger fool because he's fooling himself. Remember, no matter how carefully you sneak up on a mirror, your reflection stares right back at you. If I were in that position, I would question why my people—all of them—couldn't understand my actions.

You are not smarter than all of us. You have just enough knowledge of the law to be a highly used person. One way to check this is to break the cycle of oppressive opinions! Try seeing it from a different perspective— one that doesn't benefit the far right. This is a foolproof method for seeing the law without blinders. They commemorate you because you are instrumental in the oppression of your race. You may well go down in history as the smallest man in the jurisprudence arena. They are busy protecting their own, while you have a false vendetta against your people—a cocoon that you can operate from on the concocted pretense that we made you our enemy. You are now in so deep that you don't know the way out. Try the way that I told you about. We understand how you could be drawn into this great pit of misinformation. Four hundred years of Jim Crow will explain it all. The haters netted your a—, but you can still wake up!

This country is greater than a war on innocent people. I believe that we have a strong leader in office whose vision is far-reaching into an America that can meet the challenges of tomorrow, whether in terms of individuals' preferences that do not risk the liberties of their neighbors or the respectful recognition of a different race—

not a target of arbitrary hate schemes—by that same neighbor. I believe that America should turn a blind eye to the politicians who lack concrete purposes for the advancement of this nation. A concrete purpose in this instance would not have solid foundational material if it contained divisive components. "A house divided cannot stand" (Matt. 12:22–28).

We are fighting too many unnecessary wars at home. We have a melting pot of different races, but that is not sufficient cause to substitute understanding of each other's cultural composition for an abject rejection of that individual's existence. Respectfully we can abide by a set of laws that are not designed to keep a group of citizens in a state of system-induced poverty. The catch-22 in this situation can be a forced increase in the rate of crime merely for the sake of survival. This monster of clusterf—— becomes fodder for the politically ambitious politician to declare a platform of reducing the crime rate. To the weary neighbor who is law-abiding and is a citizen who believes in law and order, it is simple to vote this bogus, uncaring politician into office. Thus, the house becomes divided.

These thoughts that I am conveying are for the conscientious person. We know that the Jim Crows will not accept this idealistic champion of America. Hate rears its ugly head time after time, without provocation—"just because I can." Beware and be diligent in your "watch as well as pray" vigil because we didn't volunteer to get on the boat to come here. We are subject to the same misinformation that has kept us in a state of oppression for over four hundred years in this land of the free. The haters are still hating! Press on!

"What to the slave is the Fourth of July?" (Fredrick Douglass)

Book Two

Chapter Thirteen:
The Haters

The House of Representatives is in disarray. Hate is the most important business on the agenda. This is a daily menu in the year 2023. Committees and sub-committees have been formed by the far-right powers in the House with a mission to right the wrong being perpetrated upon the former POTUS, but to the knowing eyes of most citizens, it is a poorly disguised attempt to whitewash his many indictments and reduce them to what he calls a "witch hunt." Trial dates are being fought over by the prosecutors and defending counsel. Desperately the former POTUS is fighting a legal battle to regain the White House to escape conviction, for no sitting president can be arrested. Astonishingly the polls show that a vast number of voters would give this person, whom many Americans consider to be the ringleader behind the January 6 insurrection, another chance to overthrow the government.

The underlying ideology behind this movement baffles the minds of those that have a patriotic idealism about what this country should represent. That representation, to the world, is of a country of law and order. The United States promises an upstanding example of freedom and integrity. Contrary to those principles, the far right is saying we would rather crash and burn than see this freedom extended to non-White citizens. Thus this Ku-Klux-Klan would-be dictator enjoys unparalleled popularity among far-far-right pollsters.

The realization that the far right had gained control of the House had a chilling effect on the country. We had to come all this way just to see the devil's imps holding a spot for the deceiver in chief. The imps vowed to set up impeachment hearings—to oust the duly elected President of The United States. They formed committees to investigate the so-called weaponization of the government, which was aimed at the federal law enforcement community for going after their comrades in crime. A poorly organized structure ensued because their mission was flawed with uncredible evidence against their targets. Infighting and back-door deals made among themselves threatened to bring the house down around them. The ouster of one of their leaders by a handful of them left a gaping hole in the Speaker of the House position and exposed their moral ineptitude for nearly a month. After baring their clumsy incompetence to the world for three weeks, they were able to select a Speaker of the House. This leader is an outspoken election denier and was naturally endorsed by the former deceiver in chief. So we are off to the circus.

As I write, there are several indictments against the former POTUS, some stemming from the effort to overturn the 2020 election and others from visible evidence of trying to get a state election official to change the vote tally. There is one case in the state of New York where the indictment is for inflating assets in a fraudulent scheme to cheat investors (banks) and insurers. Nevertheless, his election-denier friends are plowing through with the bogus claims that there was election fraud that cost him the 2020 election.

Waiting in the wings is a somewhat more ominous figure, if that's possible. The state of Florida has its own bag of mean-spirited tricks. From the halls of Hungary comes an ideology that's rife with the smell of Nazism. The banning of books that give a history of the torturous rigors of the African American experience in America is but one sadistic act that has now become a lawful strategy to curtail our advances toward freedom and equality. The laws aimed against diversity equity and inclusion are a blatant attempt to promote discrimination, and they reek of the caste system. These nods from the government are played out in the workforce because they have been mandated by laws rubber-stamped by the state of Florida. Another racist ploy that has been exercised is the bogus gerrymandering of voting districts. This act diluted the power of African Americans to elect a candidate who would represent their interest in the state of Florida. The politician/architect/dictator who is advancing these Jim Crow laws is aspiring to be the next POTUS. If he succeeds in winning the election, chaos will ensue. We should pause for a moment and really grasp this moment in history.

There are reports that Christian evangelicals are equating the war in Israel with the coming of the Rapture—a phenomenon where the righteous will be caught up and transported to a reunion with the savior. This anticipation may well include an assumption that iniquity and, in some cases, backbiting and blatant discrimination are choices that would be accepted in such a glorious phenomenon. A pope stated that politics should not replace Christianity. This begs the question, how deep is the hate that invites the very righteous to favor the cause of dominant oppression? Another question is, have their nasty deeds down through history, which they still support, created a fear of such magnitude that they need to conjure up an understanding savior to champion their position? Would the pearly gates open to a soul who has the blood of saints upon her or his hands?

Excuse my inquisitive bent, for I have borne witness to the underlying intent to bury my people and any other non-White soul with a hate that has been handed down to you and permeates your conception of righteousness. White nationalism is your ideology, and Christianity to you is just another ingredient that you are trying to add to sweeten the concoction. So now you are rejoicing that the Speaker of the House is embracing your movement. Woe be to the downtrodden. This is what your righteous works look like as we observe your results.

The state of Florida continues to double-down on its policies of open racism in the year 2023. As was mentioned earlier in this chapter, diversity, equity, and inclusion are being legislated into laws that will cast them asunder. These laws against DEI are an attempt to overtake and overhate the front-runner for the presidential nomination within the Democratic party. The platform is a losing proposition because descendants of slaves would rather be dead than endure the oppressed state of existence that our forefathers were forced to undergo. Someone assured me that the next war would be fought between rich and poor folks. I perceive that only a handful of opportunistic Black politicians exist in the United States, but I don't see them advocating for mass genocide against minorities, and there are the rich celebrities who are of different cultural backgrounds, but they seem to be indemnified as a threat to democracy.

The mix that is before me constitutes an ever-growing extremist movement with many different names. I liken them to Hydra, the Greek mythological creature, because these groups splinter into many heads but their ideology is the same: "White supremacy."

I suspect that the January 6 extremists that have been convicted and sent to prison should examine whether they have been exploited for their dedication to a cause that only serves the purpose of a proven untrustworthy person. Many will serve time if their manipulative hero fails to win the presidential election—for there will be no pardons as promised. We descendants of slaves will have to choose life in bondage or death if the master manipulator wins. I suspect that democracy as we know it will cease to exist in these United States under his dictatorship.

Chapter Fourteen:
A Dismal Future

I know that I am painting a grim picture of the future, but I have been painting this picture since I started writing this book. There seems to be no empathy forthcoming for the middle class, nor for any class but the political class. The rich that are handling the politicians are manipulating the prices at the grocery stores to cast blame on honest politicians. It creates a voting spectacular that elects whomever the rich spend money to elect. Laws are legislated to favor the wishes of big business, and in some cases, regulatory agencies that are meant to protect the public are weakened, as with the EPA.

According to an article in the *New York Times* that appeared on January 20, 2021, the Trump administration rolled back more than one hundred environmental rules over four years. While this is but one example of the rich governing the welfare of the people, it depicts the fragility of the voters' wishes in the political arena. The smokestacks continue to smoke, spewing their poison into the atmosphere, and the Flint River keeps supplying poisoned water to the poor folks in Michigan. Yet we consumers run to and fro in search of a savior. The man that rolled back those environmental regulations is favored to win the Republican nomination to run for the President of The United States. We are again neither mute nor amazed. But we still vote in quest of a change. The question of reality comes into play when the races are after each other's throats because of the misinformation being fed to them.

The unimaginable hell that is upon the people in Gaza at this time is greater than the hell visited upon the Israelis by Hamas terrorists when they carried out a raid on Israel's soil. There have been reports of war crimes by the Israeli army upon civilians within Gaza. We do well to take note of the lack of empathy among our Americans for the carnage that is perpetrated on women and even babies during this war of vengeance. There are those in these United States that are advocating the same for people of color. This is a time to see reality and to wake up to the possibilities of mass genocide. A dictator might try to carry out such a horrendous endeavor. The whole world is calling for Israel to cease and desist. They have vowed to continue until the last Hamas terrorist is eradicated. The cost is thousands of innocent people being slaughtered.

Fascist rhetoric comparable to Hitler's and Mussolini's calls for an authoritarian government is now embraced by the front-runner for the Republican nomination. This rhetoric is not new, but the language is stronger. Prominent leaders in both parties are warning the country of this dangerous bent toward fascism. The name Victor Orbán surfaces again from the lips of a would-be dictator. He was mentioned earlier in this book in connection with a GOP candidate for POTUS from the great state of Florida. The rhetoric that is being touted points toward the eradication of non-White nationalists. Words spoken include "vermin" and "poisoning the blood of our country." Supporters of this rhetoric downplay it as innocent jargon, but wise leaders of our country know that these excerpts from Hitler's speeches are a thrust toward fascism. He who has ears let him hear.

This fascist direction is not new for this presidential candidate. A long history of racist policies in business and lawsuits for housing discrimination follows this would-be dictator. Astute in business, he has been able to recruit the far right to be a strong arm in his quest to eradicate the United States Constitution. Threats of retaliation with a hint of violence against the disciples of democracy from the would-be dictator have been reported. The sight of him hugging an extremist who was involved in the January 6 riot was telling. What I find to be amazing is the assumption that he will be running as the Republican candidate for president in the 2024 election. There are a total of ninety-one indictments against him, and some of them amount to an attempt to mount an insurrection against the United States Government.

President Abraham Lincoln warned of the possibility that the country could be vulnerable to destruction from internal forces. The Constitution is now teetering on a dangerous precipice of totalitarian government, and democracy is being challenged by idiots—in a crazy game of roulette. The military now has become part of a political ploy to promote senseless ideologies against women's rights. There is a movie titled *Ship of Fools*…again, we are neither mute nor amazed because there is smoke on the horizon from fires burning in the so-called innocent pulpits of those who falsely proclaim values that they purport are superior to those of every other race. These so-called superior values have so many miles on them that they would do well to be overhauled. These so-called values are not so cleverly disguised Eurocentric thrusts toward domination on the world stage. They are supporting ideologies of oppression. They are not supporting true Christianity as hate is not Christlike.

Chapter Fifteen:
Axis of Evil

The not-so-apolitical Supreme Court will make some very important constitutional decisions during the next two years. There is a push toward totalitarian government by powerful components of the legislature and the front-runner of the Republican party. The fate of the country hangs in the balance. In the House there are those who fight to keep the government from passing a budget that doesn't support their mean-spirited ideologies, such as antiabortion legislation. The idea that a Speaker of the House would negotiate with his Democratic counterpart is a dangerous one for him. A subcommittee that is spending the taxpayers' money on frivolous ventures such as going after prosecutors and law officers that dare to go after those whose platform is to overthrow the government and eradicate the provisions of the Constitution.

The latest threat to the Voting Rights Act happened when The Eighth Circuit Court of Appeals ruled that only the US government can sue under a landmark civil rights law barring racial discrimination in voting. The appeals court maintains that a key provision in the 1965 Voting Rights Act provides that only the Department of Justice can file a discrimination suit. This case will be heading to the SCOTUS, and I believe it will be one of the most important cases that will be heard by the court. Voters are easily swayed. Here is a landmark event that shows how easy it is.

The Nathaniel Bacon rebellion resulted in the first known incidence in the United States of using skin color for discriminatory practices. Nathaniel Bacon was a noncommissioned ward of the colony of Virginia. He proposed to the governor that the colony should be eradicated of all Indians. Governor Berkely balked at this proposal because he feared that it would prompt all the Indians to revolt against them. At that time the colonies were still under British rule. Nathaniel Bacon was able to organize Black slaves and Black freedmen, as well as White indentured servants, into a rebellious group. He then rebelled against Governor Berkely and overpowered the governor's protective forces. This rebellion failed when the government started giving the White indentured servants more benefits. These recipients ceased to participate after their fortunes were adjusted. Their status was raised significantly by the government over that of people of African descent. To distinguish the recipients of the benefits, the Africans were deemed to be called Black, and the indentured servants were identified as White. This resulted in a so-called legitimate reason to discriminate against the Black people whether they were freedmen or slaves.

In the upcoming elections of 2024, voters will be enticed to vote with a far-right candidate regardless of his fascist characteristics or his blatant attempts to bring the United States Constitution down. History has taught us that there have been more lynchings of African Americans during inflationary times in these United States than at any other time. He who has ears let him hear: these are inflationary times! Why would a candidate who has ninety-one indictments against him be the leading candidate in the polls for the Republican party? It seems to be ridiculously improbable but remains a reality. It is also unbelievable but true that women have been burned alive in these United States on no evidence except the superstitious belief that they were witches.

Voting rights are being challenged mightily because freedom is a barrier against autocracy. All Americans should fear this thrust toward fascism, as we have evidence in the Holocaust of the results. The promises of programs against the advancement of minorities and immigrants are a repeat of what happened after the Nathaniel Bacon rebellion. The autocrat's playbook contains excerpts from Victor Orbán of Hungary—a devout racist.

Have I said enough to convince you that we need everyone to vote their conscience? As stated earlier, there are factions in the House of Representatives that will support the fascist ideology of the would-be dictator because they are unable to seize power for themselves—they would be content to ride the coattails of a power-hungry madman into the jaws of hell even if it meant taking America the beautiful down with them. My plea is a simple and familiar one: VOTE! A persistent problem that we have can be described in an old cliché: "Don't throw the baby out with the bathwater!" We have a president who is trying to keep our best interest at the forefront. The far-right isn't making any promises that we will be represented in any of their racist policies. They are promising that we will again be shoved down into Jim-Crow, subordinate, second-class citizenship—scratching and clawing for the right to call them master.

I know that the polls are showing a dissatisfaction among African American voters with the current administration. Having been around for seventy-eight years, I can tell you Jim Crow laws have been more hideous than what we have now. We have a president that is pulled in many directions currently with the volatile situations on the world stage, support for two wars, and far-right antagonists nipping at his heels like jackals trying to find an opening to his vulnerable underbelly. What is unimaginable is the many far-right citizens embracing this concept of hate in the United States. I think that a vast number of them are bloodthirsty zealots praying for mass genocide upon those who are not them. I base this assumption on the January 6 riot in our nation's capital. They would have senselessly killed innocent people that day.

I have a plan. Instead of complaining, we could help ourselves and him by voting. We could further help ourselves by pooling our resources and talent to strengthen ourselves. A rope is stronger when it has more strands. We need to figure out how to stop the war between our young men. We need to be searching for the truth about our past. Someone is trying hard to block the truth. This may be a starting point because this seems to be extremely important, judging from the laws enacted.

The old devil is not mincing words about seeking and destroying those who stood up to him. The power of citizens going to the polls and voting has him sitting on the sidelines at the present time. If he is allowed to return to power, it would take a civil war to get him out again. I have pleaded for unity and model of voting in the book *The Alternative Truth*. Once is not enough to defeat this type of dragon. He is cunning in the ways of summoning the age-old power of Jim Crow from the ashes of the black codes. From there he has found enough sparks to resurrect old moldy Jim Crow, who had been as dormant as Vesuvius. Now we have a nation of domestic terrorists. They are threatening every race, color, creed, religion, and nationality that isn't them. The would-be autocrat is carefully stoking the fires of dictatorship. He who has eyes, let him see! Throughout the hierarchy of the courts and the government, he has demons in place to do his bidding. Again, our kryptonite is the voting booth. That is our fire truck in case of fire—vote!

I can begin to explain the reason for the violence that our young men are visiting upon each other. I know there is an underlying cause. It is frustrating to see it being played out across the nation. We are saying stop; we need you. The problem is that we fear we will become part of the problem by trying to defend our own lives if we approach them. It has gotten to this level. No one came to their rescue when the ghettoes were flooded with drugs, alcohol, and guns. Violence is the product of this volatile mix. This is my assessment of the situation. After this plan of destruction by someone with diabolical intentions of mass genocide, which includes destroying the lives of our youth, the stage is set for the biggest gang in the United States to move in and mop up. These big gang members, wearing honest-looking blue, are being financed by the same entities that set the stage with the concoction of drugs, alcohol, and guns. Again, the answer is at the polls. We need to participate in the fight for our freedom. Our very lives are at stake.

The election of 2024 looms large, and factions are gearing up to place their ugly hatred upon the weary backs of the have-nots of these United States. There will be those who will vote against their own welfare. They will vote for the eradication of the Constitution. They will vote for the eradication of freedom. They will vote blindly for Orbán's convoluted ideology.

Meanwhile, the raw hatred that men seem to enjoy as a sport is running its course in America.

I must reiterate the important fact that hate in America is a vehicle to promote the sport of lynchings. These lynchings are most often perpetrated on people of color's minds and bodies. Embraced by so-called Christian White nationalists, the hypocrisy of law and order as a platform to seek dictatorship is promised by a politician who is under ninety-one indictments. We descendants of slaves remain the overall targets of these lies. Long gone is Willie Lynch, but his teachings are still a part of the vehicle of hate in America. Lest we forget the horrors that lurk just beneath the surface of yesterday, we only have to revisit the lynching of Mary Turner.

The lynching of our minds comes in the form of an antiwoke campaign that is designed to mask the resurrection of the black codes. Redlining, gerrymandering, and gentrification are also tools of racism. Critical race theory—a racist-busting endeavor by brilliant scholars—has exposed the loopholes in the legal system that are used to circumvent our rights by the introduction of so-called superior laws that supposedly supersede our civil rights. These are countermeasures to our quest for equality.

Diversity, equity, and inclusion have now become illegal according to the far-right super bigots. The tenant farmers lived through it all by just pressing on against the odds. Those that could escape to the Northern states did so, only to discover that hate in America had no boundaries. Rat-infested slums owned by rich bigots became the box canyon of despair that was their welcome home, their respite from the lynch mobs of the South— led by the fabled big-belly sheriff.

The sum total is a Eurocentric devil-may-care thrust toward world domination in opposition to an Afrocentric quest for freedom and equality. It can be likened to an irresistible force against an immovable object. The voting booth awaits! It is the antidote in case of hate!

Book Three

Chapter Sixteen:
The Haters

It's uncanny—or maybe it's ordered by some unseen force—that evil can escape reckoning while shaping dire futures for the innocent and unsuspecting people of this earth. I have met the monsters, and they are unforgiving. Machiavellian, they are cunning. Narcissists, they have a knack for grandiosity and a need to feel superior. Psychopaths, they are unable to feel remorse for criminal infractions. They feel that they have the privilege to take the lion's share of anything worth having. These monsters are openly proclaiming a dystopian state for the rest of us. They are the epitome of the properties of the dark triad listed above. The Machiavellian trait denotes a cunning, calculating mind; this group wants to be your friend. The psychopath will not socialize with you. The narcissist frowns down at you. Together they are quite formidable. They hate anyone that doesn't accept their ideology. They are seeking a cultural shift, and they are willing to spend whatever they have gained—even the freedoms guaranteed in the Constitution—for the right to not have to share that freedom. Old Jim Crow is their dear grandfather, and they are nostalgic for the days when they could walk on someone.

It deeply saddens me to see the beginning of destruction coming to a nation that so many have died for. The super bigot isn't worth it! Right-thinking people are asking themselves why. What concoction is so strong and compelling that it can hide the lies that are in plain view? What manner of Jim Crow witchcraft is this? The answer is the same age-old answer. Racism! It can be achieved if enough voters want it. After this time, they won't have to worry about anything else again, he promises. He will handle everything. Our votes have never been more important. I hope to see you at the polls!